What's in this book

学习内容 Contents   2

读一读 Read   4

听听说说 Listen and say   12

写一写 Write   16

多元学习 Connections   18

温习 Checkpoint   20

分享 Sharing   22

This book belongs to

_____

超人爸爸 Superdad

学习内容 Contents

沟通 Communication

向他人道早
Greet people in the morning

向他人打招呼
Greet people at any time of the day

向他人道别
Say goodbye to people

生词 New words

★ 早　good morning

★ 你好　hello

★ 再见　goodbye

爸爸　father, dad

妈妈　mother, mum

浩浩　Hao Hao

句式 Sentence patterns

爸爸，早！ Good morning, Dad!

浩浩，你好！ Hello, Hao Hao!

妈妈，再见！ Goodbye, Mum!

跨学科学习 Project

制作手偶，问候他人
Make a hand puppet and say
hello and goodbye

文化 Cultures

中国人打招呼的方式
Chinese ways of greetings

Get ready

1 What do you do before you go to sleep?

2 What story is Mum reading to Hao Hao?

3 Does Hao Hao like the story?

爸爸，早！妈妈，早！

浩浩，再见！

超人，你好！

你好！爸爸送我上学。

谢谢爸爸。再见!

浩浩，早。上学了。

Let's think

1 How does Hao Hao usually go to school? Trace the correct line.

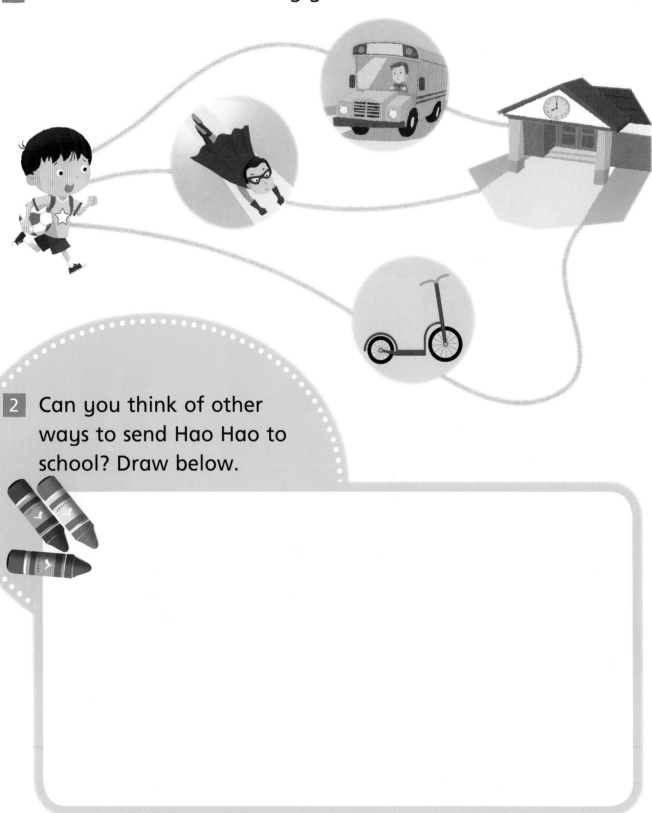

2 Can you think of other ways to send Hao Hao to school? Draw below.

New words

1 Learn the new words.

2 Match the words to the pictures. Write the letters.

a 早   b 再见   c 你好

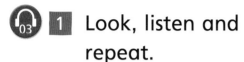 听听说说 Listen and say

🎧 03 **1** Look, listen and repeat.

1

2

3

🎧 04 **2** Look at the pictures. Listen to the stor

① 浩浩，早。上学了！

妈妈，早！

③ 浩浩，早！

早，妈妈送我上学！

nd say.

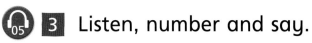

Task

Speak Chinese to your friends. Write their names and tick when you have done so.

	早！	你好！	再见！
Hao Hao	✓	✓	✓
1			
2			
3			

Game

Listen to your teacher. Find the way out of the crocodile pond.

Song

🎧 06 Listen and sing.

早上好，早上好，

爸爸妈妈早上好！

我去上学说再见，

爸爸妈妈说再见！

课堂用语 Classroom language

看	听	说	读	写	画
look	listen	say	read	write	draw

写一写 Write

1 Learn and trace the strokes.

横

竖

2 Learn the component. Circle 日 in the characters.

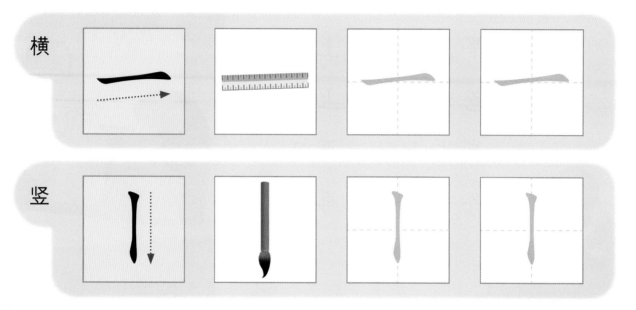

日　早　时　晨　星

3 Colour the suns and draw arrows to shoot down two of them.

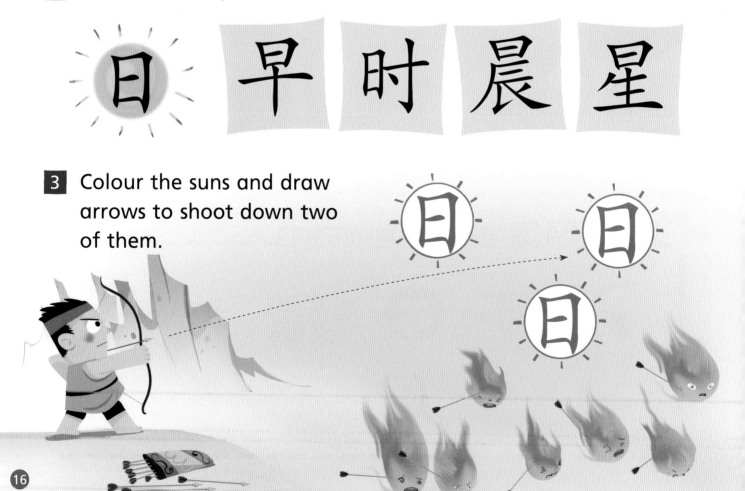

4 Trace and write the character.

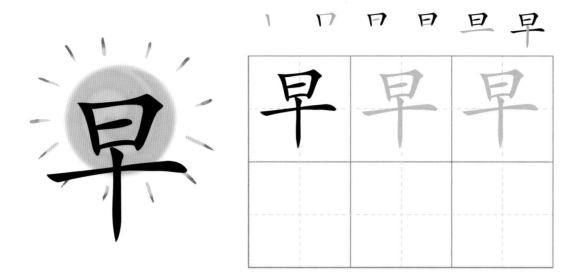

`ノ  冂 冂 日 旦 早`

早	早	早

5 Write and say.

![ ] **!**   ![ ] **!**

汉字小常识 Did you know?

Colour the upper component red and the lower component green.

> Some characters are made up of upper and lower components.

早	爸	见	看	写

Cultures

1 Do you know how Chinese people greet each other?

In old China, people greeted each other in this way.

Now, Chinese adults shake hands when they meet.

Children usually wave their hands.

2 How do you greet people? Draw on the right.

你好! 你好!

Project

1 Make an ice lolly hand puppet.

Be careful with the scissors!

2 Say hello and goodbye to your friends.

......

你好!

再见!

早!

温习 Checkpoint

1 Play the board game.

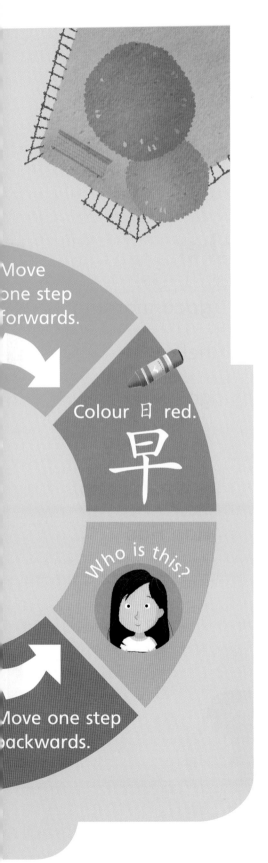

Move one step forwards.

Colour 日 red.

早

Who is this?

Move one step backwards.

2 Work with your friend. Colour the stars and the chillies.

Words and sentences	说	读	写
早	☆	☆	☆
你好	☆	☆	🌶
再见	☆	☆	🌶
爸爸，早！	☆	🌶	🌶
妈妈，再见！	☆	🌶	🌶
浩浩，你好！	☆	🌶	🌶

Greet people in the morning	☆
Greet people at any time of the day	☆
Say goodbye to people	☆

3 What does your teacher say?

My teacher says ...

分享 Sharing

Words I remember

早	zǎo	good morning
你好	nǐ hǎo	hello
再见	zài jiàn	goodbye
爸爸	bà ba	father, dad
妈妈	mā ma	mother, mum
浩浩	hào hao	Hao Hao

Other words

超人	chāo rén	superman
送	sòng	to take
我	wǒ	I, me
上学	shàng xué	to go to school
谢谢	xiè xie	thanks

OXFORD
UNIVERSITY PRESS

Oxford University Press is a department of the University of Oxford.
It furthers the University's objective of excellence in research, scholarship,
and education by publishing worldwide. Oxford is a registered trade mark of
Oxford University Press in the UK and in certain other countries

Published in Hong Kong by
Oxford University Press (China) Limited
39th Floor, One Kowloon, 1 Wang Yuen Street, Kowloon Bay,
Hong Kong

Illustrated by Anne Lee and Wildman

Photographs for reproduction permitted by Dreamstime.com

China National Publications Import & Export (Group) Corporation is an authorized distributor of
Oxford Elementary Chinese.

Please contact content@cnpiec.com.cn or 86-10-65856782

ISBN: 978-0-19-942968-4

10 9 8 7 6 5 4 3 2